Desert Fox

by Nat Gabriel
•
illustrated by
Sally Wern Comport

Scott Foresman

Editorial Offices: Glenview, Illinois • New York, New York
Sales Offices: Reading, Massachusetts • Duluth, Georgia
Glenview, Illinois • Carrollton, Texas • Menlo Park, California

The sun comes up.

It is hot.
Who is around?
Look!

3

The old fox comes out.

She is hot.
She looks all around.

She needs water.
She finds some!

She needs food too.
She finds some.

But it is too hot to hunt.
It is too hot to run.
It is too hot to be out in the sun.

8

It is time to sleep.
She finds a spot.
She naps.

9

The sun goes down.
The old fox wakes up.
She goes out.

She looks around.
It is cool now.
It is time to hunt.

Her ears help her.
Her eyes help her.
The old fox sees a lizard.

First she hides.
She looks.
She waits.

Next she runs around.

Then she jumps on it.
It can not run away.

It is time to eat.
The sun comes up again.